EASY SOLOS

FOR CLARINET, TRUMPET, OR TENOR SAX

CONTENTS

To access audio visit:
www.halleonard.com/mylibrary

Enter Code
4229-8877-9938-7762

ISBN 978-1-59615-238-0

EXCLUSIVELY DISTRIBUTED BY

7777 W. BLUEMOUND RD. P.O. BOX 13819 MILWAUKEE, WI 53213

Visit Hal Leonard Online at
www.halleonard.com

Beautiful Isle Of Somewhere

JOHN S. FEARIS

To A Wild Rose

4 beats (2 measures)
precede music.

EDWARD MACDOWELL, Op. 51

Track 2

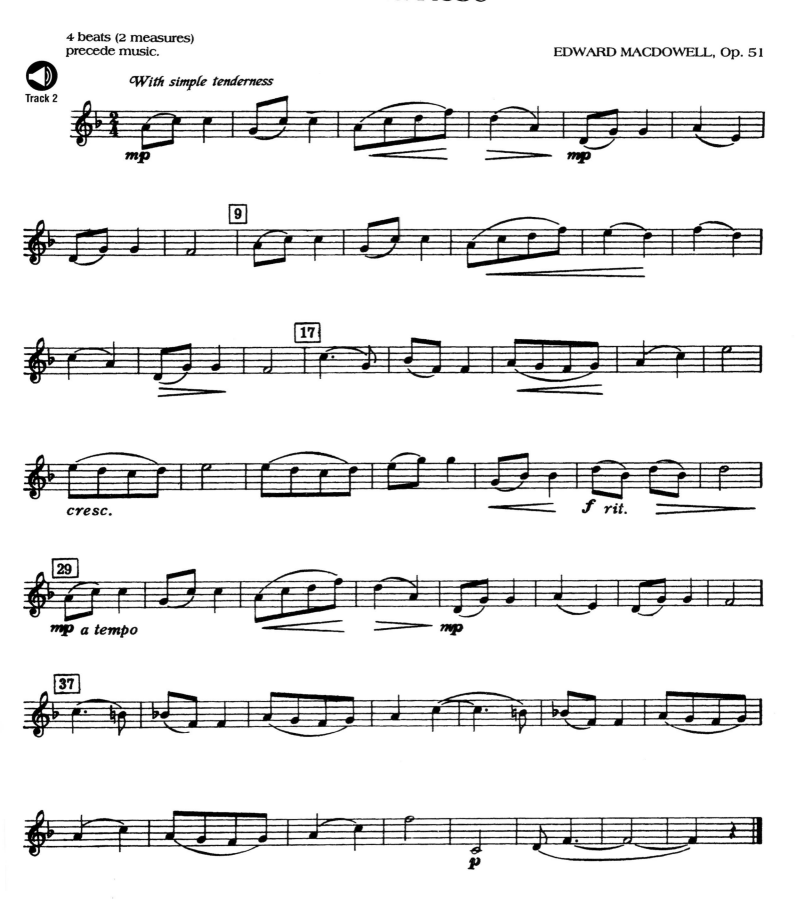

4

Daisy Bell
(A Bicycle Built for Two)

HARRY DACRE

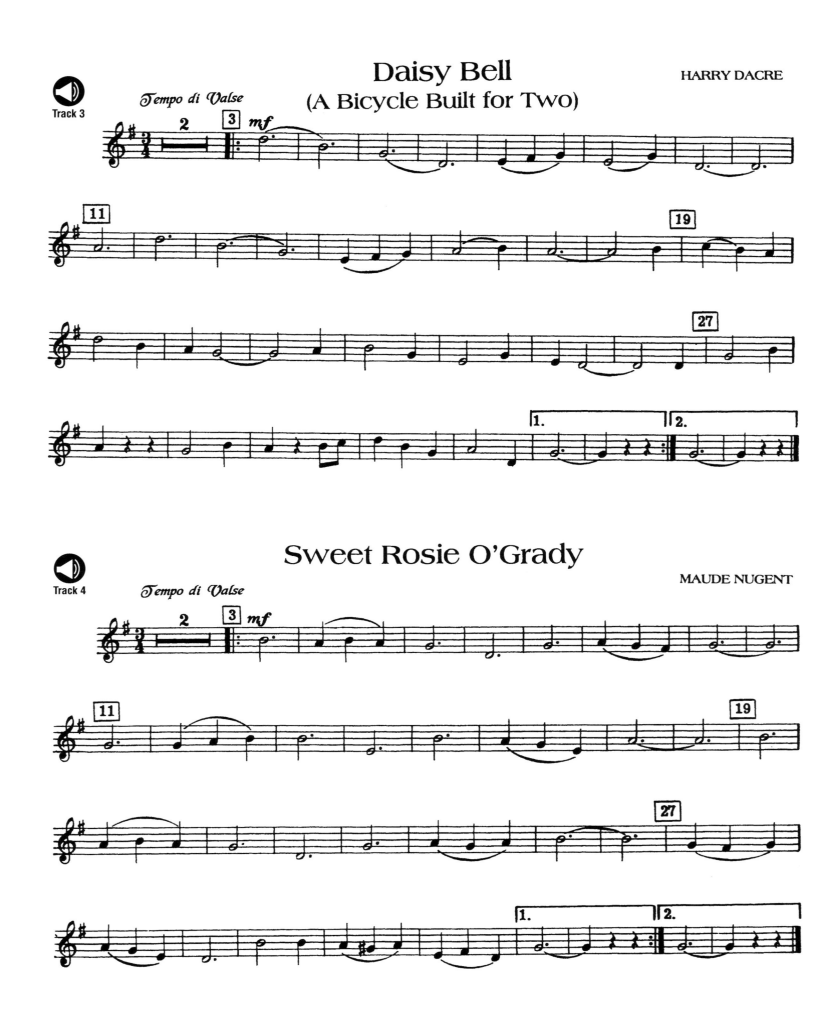

Sweet Rosie O'Grady

MAUDE NUGENT

Pomp And Circumstance

EDWARD ELGAR

Mighty Lak' A Rose

ETHELBERT NEVIN

Kentucky Babe

ADAM GEIBEL

Track 7

The Band Played On

CHARLES E. WARD

Track 8

After The Ball

CHARLES K. HARRIS

Track 9

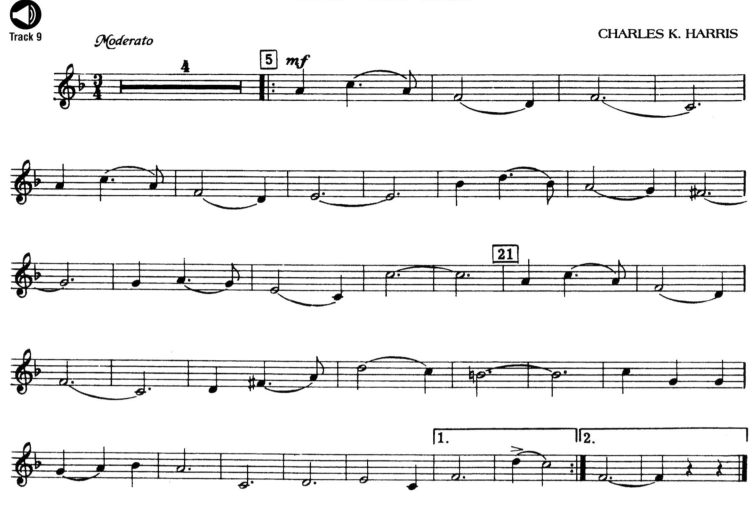

Santa Lucia

Neapolitan Song

Track 10

Red River Valley

Track 11

Cowboy Song

Kathleen Mavourneen

Track 12

FREDERICK N. CROUCH

10

America, The Beautiful

3 beats (3/4 measure) precede music.

SAMUEL A. WARD

Track 13

Hatikvoh
(The Hope)

4 beats (1 measure) precede music.

Hebrew National Anthem

Track 14

American Patrol

F. W. MEACHAM

Battle Hymn Of The Republic

JULIA WARD HOWE

3 beats plus 1 silent precede music.

I'll Sing Thee Songs Of Araby

FREDERIC CLAY

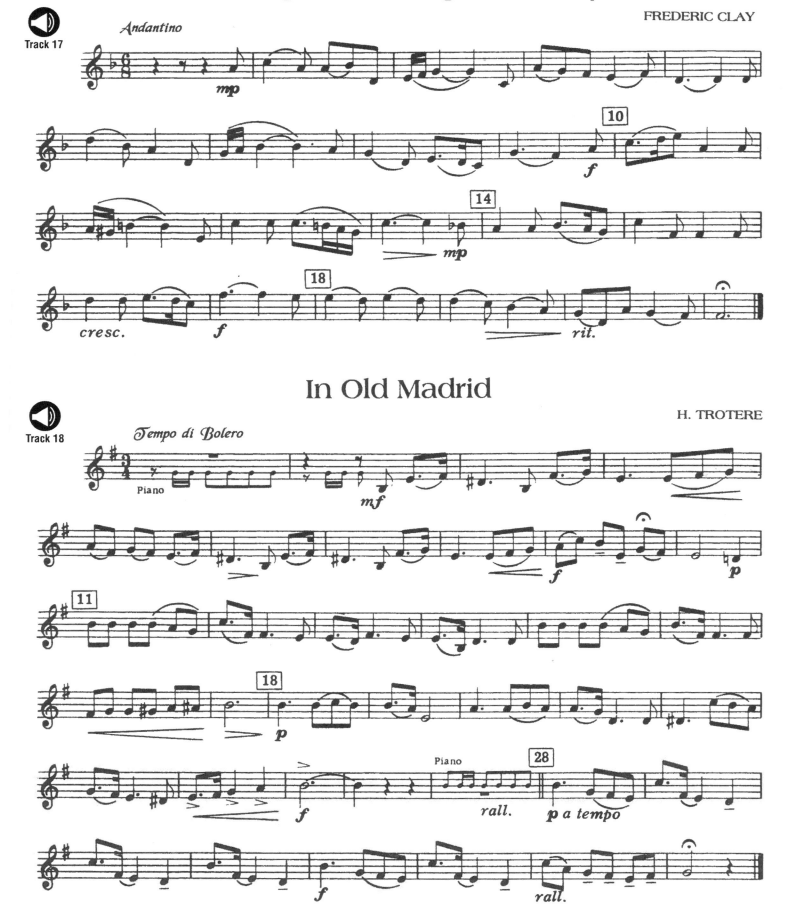

In Old Madrid

H. TROTERE

O Sole Mio!

E. DE CAPUA

La Paloma

SEBASTIAN YRADIER

La Spagnola

VINCENZO DI CHIARA

3 beats (1 measure)
precede music.

Tempo di Valse

Track 21

La Cumparsita

4 beats (2 measures)
precede music.

G. H. MATOS RODERIGUEZ

Track 22

Adios Muchachos

CARLOS SANDERS

El Choclo

A. G. VILLOLDO

Oh Promise Me

Track 25

The Rosary

4 beats (1 measure)
precede music.

Track 27

Lento

ETHELBERT NEVIN

Just A-Wearyin' For You

Track 28

CARRIE JACOBS-BOND

I Love You Truly

Track 29

CARRIE JACOBS-BOND

Vilia
(from "The Merry Widow")

FRANZ LEHAR

Track 30

Gypsy Love Song
(from "The Fortune Teller")

VICTOR HERBERT

Track 32

Slowly

Piano   mf

10

14

rit.   a tempo   rit.

Marche Slave

P.I. TSCHAIKOWSKY, Op. 31

Track 33

Moderato   3 espressivo

Piano   mp

11

19

27

f

3

Ah! So Pure
(from "Martha")

FRIEDRICH VON FLOTOW

Track 34

Eili, Eili

Track 35

3 beats (1 measure)
precede music.

Hebrew Melody

Who Is Sylvia?

FRANZ SCHUBERT

Theme
(from Piano Concerto, Op. 16)

EDVARD GRIEG

Song Of India

N. RIMSKY-KORSAKOFF

Track 38

Serenade

VICTOR HERBERT

Track 39

Finlandia

JEAN SIBELIUS

Theme
(from Piano Concerto, No. 2, Op. 18)

SERGEI RACHMANINOFF

Für Elise

5 beats plus 4 soft beats
(3 meas.) precede music.

LUDWIG VAN BEETHOVEN

Fantasie Impromptu
(Theme)

FREDERIC CHOPIN, Op. 66

Track 43

Mexican Hat Dance

4 beats (2 measures)
set tempo.

F. A. PARTICHELA

Track 44

The Glow Worm

PAUL LINCKE

MORE GREAT SAXOPHONE PUBLICATIONS FROM

Music Minus One

ADVANCED ALTO SAX SOLOS – VOLUME 1

Performed by Paul Brodie, alto saxophone
Accompaniment: Antonin Kubalek, piano

Virtuoso Paul Brodie introduces you to the world of advanced alto sax solos with this wide-ranging collection. Contains performance suggestions and Mr. Brodie's incredible interpretations to help you achieve greatness! Includes a printed music score containing the solo part, annotated with performance suggestions; and access to professional recordings with complete versions (with soloist) followed by piano accompaniments to each piece, minus the soloist. Includes works by Vivaldi, Jacob, Whitney, and Benson.

00400602 Book/Online Audio $16.99

ADVANCED ALTO SAX SOLOS – VOLUME 2

Performed by Vincent Abato, alto saxophone
Accompaniment: Harriet Wingreen, piano

Listen as extraordinary virtuoso Vincent Abato of the Metropolitan Opera Orchestra takes you further into the advanced repertoire with these spectacular sax selections. Listen to his masterful interpretations, examine his performance suggestions, then you step in and make magic with Harriet Wingreen, legendary piano accompanist for the New York Philharmonic. Includes: Schubert "The Bee," Rabaud "Solo de Concours," and Creston "Sonata, Op. 19" 2nd and 3rd movements. Includes a printed music score containing the solo part, annotated with performance suggestions; and tracks with complete versions (with soloist) followed by piano accompaniments to each piece, minus the soloist.

00400603 Book/Online Audio $16.99

PLAY THE MUSIC OF BURT BACHARACH
ALTO OR TENOR SAXOPHONE

Along with lyricist Hal David, Burt Bacharach penned some of the best pop songs and standards of all time. These superb collections let solo instrumentalists play along with: Alfie • Blue on Blue • Do You Know the Way to San Jose • I Say a Little Prayer • Magic Moments • This Guy's in Love with You • Walk on By • What the World Needs Now • The Windows of the World • and Wives and Lovers.

00400657 Book/Online Audio $22.99

BOSSA, BONFÁ & BLACK ORPHEUS FOR TENOR SAXOPHONE – A TRIBUTE TO STAN GETZ
TENOR SAXOPHONE

featuring Glenn Zottola

Original transcriptions for you to perform! The bossa novas that swept the world in 1950 created a whole new set of songs to equal the great standards of the '20s, '30s and '40s by Gershwin, Porter, Arlen, Berlin, Kern and Rodgers. This collection for tenor sax is a tribute to the great Stan Getz and includes: Black Orpheus • Girl from Ipanema • Gentle Rain • One Note Samba • Once I Loved • Dindi • Baubles, Bangles and Beads • Meditation • Triste • I Concentrate on You • Samba de Orfeu.

00124387 Book/Online Audio $16.99

CLASSIC STANDARDS FOR ALTO SAXOPHONE
A TRIBUTE TO JOHNNY HODGES

featuring Bob Wilber

Ten classic standards are presented in this book as they were arranged for the Neal Heft String Orchestra in 1954, including: Yesterdays • Laura • What's New? • Blue Moon • Can't Help Lovin' Dat Man • Embraceable You • Willow Weep for Me • Memories of You • Smoke Gets in Your Eyes • Stardust. Bob Wilber performs the songs on the provided CD on soprano saxophone, although they are translated for alto saxophone.

00131389 Book/Online Audio $16.99

EASY JAZZ DUETS FOR 2 ALTO SAXOPHONES AND RHYTHM SECTION

Performed by Hal McKusick, alto saxophone
Accompaniment: The Benny Goodman Rhythm Section: George Duvivier, bass; Bobby Donaldson, drums

This great collection of jazz duets gives you the opportunity accompany saxophonist Hal McKusick and the Benny Goodm Rhythm Section. Suitable for beginning players, all the selecti are great fun. This album allows you to play either duet pa Includes printed musical score with access to online audio trac you hear both parts played in stereo, then each duet is repea with the first part omitted and then the second part, so you can play along.

00400480 Book/Online Audio ....$16.

FROM DIXIE TO SWING
CLARINET OR SOPRANO SAX

Performed by Kenny Davern, clarinet
Accompaniment: Kenny Davern, clarinet & soprano sax; 'Do Cheatham, trumpet; Vic Dickenson, trombone; Dick Wellsto piano; George Duvivier, bass; Gus Johnson Jr., drums

Such jazz legends as Dick Wellstood, Alphonse 'Doc' Cheatham a George Duvivier and more back you up in this amazing collecti of New York-style Dixieland standards. After the break-up of big-band era around 1950, many of the finest 'swing' or ma stream players found themselves without an outlet for their abili and took to playing 'Dixieland' in New York clubs such as Eddie Condon's and the Metropo And so was born a new style of Dixieland jazz minus the banjos, tubas, steamboats and m nolias! It is this version we celebrate on this album. We encourage you, the soloist, to inve counter-melodies rather than mere harmony parts. This is a music of loose weaving parts, one of precision ensemble figures. And in short, it is one of the greatest improvisational ex riences any jazz player could hope to have. Includes a printed music score and online aud access to stereo accompaniments to each piece.

00400613 Book/Online Audio ....$16.

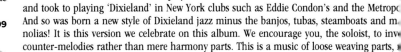

GLAZUNOV – CONCERTO IN E-FLAT MAJOR, OP. 109; VON KOCH – CONCERTO IN E-FLAT MAJOR
ALTO SAXOPHONE

Performed by Lawrence Gwozdz, alto saxophone
Accompaniment: Plovdiv Philharmonic Orchestra
Conductor: Nayden Todorov

Alexander Glazunov, one of the great masters of late Russi Romanticism, was fascinated by the saxophone and by ja In 1934 he wrote this beautiful saxophone concerto which h become a classic, combining romanticism with modern idioms well. Erland von Koch's 1958 saxophone concerto is filled with experimental modern tona ties and fantastic effects for the saxophone. Both are must-haves for the serious saxophc ist. Includes a printed music score; informative liner notes; and online audio featuring concerti performed twice: first with soloist, then again with orchestral accompaniment on minus you, the soloist. The audio is accessed online using the unique code inside each bc and can be streamed or downloaded.

00400487 Book/Online Audio ....$16.

To see a full listing of Music Minus One publications, visit
www.halleonard.com/MusicMinusOne

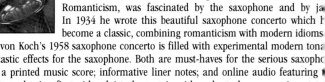

Prices, contents, and availability subject to change without notice.

07
3